FURTHER WEST & FIREWEED

POEMS BY
LANCEE WHETMAN

A WATERMARKED SMILE
TO ALL THE PLACES I HAVE LEFT BEHIND
IN CONTINUAL PURSUIT OF MYSELF.

TO THE CHASERS-OF-THE-QUIET

TABLE OF CONTENTS

OPENING LINES TO MY MEMOIR

Something I've failed to mention: Hopefulness. It looks nice but doesn't actually function (just yet). I am my biggest nay-sayer. A budding icon raised on desert adobe and static Tim McGraw tunes, still possessing a last name from my now-estranged father. A June Gemini undergoing a calm change-of-heart—a fascinating contradiction. Time will tell if it all really is significant or not. My personal revolution holds huge promise (I think). I've been learning the power of the "pivot" (heard it on a Ted Talk recently), transitioning from law to lawlessness. My resistant properties are starting to wane (this thrifted Gore-Tex is getting old), and I am permeating straight through to my own goddamn heart. I'm being pushed to move forward toward success (even though I am scared of it). Taking on the very obligatory kind of self-experimentation (though I haven't dyed my hair blonde yet—it's on the bucket list). Emerging in fields of ecstasy and morning mountain mist, I'm coming clean—no complacency. Capturing my own firefly desire, bottled up, dreaming big now, racing my stallion heart toward wilder pursuits. Sprigs of lilac on the dashboard, harvesting a Hail Mary transformation. Along the way, I'll keep reading an array of opening lines of books I'll never buy, putting sound to syllable, and allow myself to imagine that I am something great.

HI HO, HI HO, IT'S OFF TO WORK WE GO

Day in, day out
Day out, day in
The monotony of repetitious keyboard clacking
An introvert's inclination against interaction
Promising punctuality, punching-in, Punk'd by capitalism.
A dreary deadline always looming, hardly life-affirming.
Paper-filing fears humming the
Hi ho, hi ho, it's off to work we go song
With nine-to-five's and
Wasting away the days-of-our-lives
Cut the cubicle bullshit
Unplug.
Now offline and

out of service.

THE OFFICE

I am the epitome of professionalism. Hair: double Frenched. Ears: double-pierced. Attire: Mustard-colored corduroy pants, long-legged floods, a few inches too high, peeping ankles. A fleece burgundy-lined pullover, knock-off Patagucci (i.e., Patagonia). Gray, on-sale Costco wool socks (bought in bulk), mid-calf height. Hipster-wannabe Birkenstocks, brown blobs strapping me in for the nine-to-five ride, blazing through the office corridors (comfily), cushioning my plantar-fasciitis plagued feet. File-cabinet filing my unmanicured nails—*found the paper I was looking for!* Hands up, this roller-coaster cubicle can get a little crazy in this unrecyclable life, the big paper-shuffle. A pack of Marlboro cigarettes on a 15-minute smoke break, I'm coughing up stress-free zones. Like clockwork, it's time to make a "living." Microsoft Teams chat dinging—PING! Meeting in five. Eye-strain alert, *where'd I put my blue-light glasses?* Basking in bleak overhead-paneled lighting—*where's my happy lamp?* Unlabeled food in the refrigerator, *I forgot my lunch.* Take a first-story noon escape for ramen's rescue again. Shackled to QWERTY-typed orders. Bargaining with the boss over time off for a vacation. Swivel-chair procrastination, fire-alarm break. *You've-got-mail!* Oh shit, it's a termination letter: *Fired.*

(At least now I'm free).

No more living life in list form.
No more desk-job daydreaming.
Just another hippie without healthcare.
Further west,
Here I come.

BADGE OF COURAGE

I told you so is a frequent maxim in leaving's initial struggle.
Staunch forewarnings of foul-weather windows on the way—
we never did quite forecast change brilliantly.
There's nectar and needing in chasing foreign acres
when certain rendered pain resides in the same places
we also hold so dearly—
equidistant from epiphany's cure and stagnancy's predictability
coddling maybe-one-day wounds never earned a medal of honor.
But, when the woman-I-want-to-be visits,
she cradles these departure insecurities and,
soothsayer-like,
disquiets fear.
Do the damn thing already.
Go.
She soaks the word *stay* in river's renewal—
it is washed away like a stubborn stain
dipped in bygone birthplace bleach.
In a honey-breathing sigh and fresh air's tender vigor,
I gaze toward spring's mosaic of just-budding tulips
tempted, evermore,
by the call of horizon's commemorative glances.
Please forgive me for the news that'll reach you,
dear mother,
in dawn's gracious grin,
of my tidings.
For I am crossing state lines in
miles and miles of merriment,
so alive and so well-rested—
always playing with shiny objects,
the western sun
gleaming like a badge of courage.

TO BEREAVE A PAST SELF

Lassoed and lost
confiding in earth's labyrinth
running at an unmanageable pace
away from thunder-driven thwarting-of-plans.
Do I betray my birthplace
abandoning *home* like this?
Storming Capricorn no longer dots the night
and I take shelter in fallen petals.
Stagnation's bitter pulp tastes like a sip
Of a moving-on mosquito mojito—
blood-sucking on transitionary tonics.
Charring wood for a dim-lit soul
chimney smoke rising with the afterlife.
Unsettled by nettle's stinging leaf—
symbolism perhaps?
Can I dress in all black in the next world?
There's *fun* in funeral, right?
Summoned by cypress canopies
that out lean their silhouettes to see me.
Save me.
Unaware to the current moon-phase predilections
all I know is that
right now,
I am looking for solace
to bereave my former self
in peace.

BITTERSWEET GRATEFULNESS

Sorry if I'm starting to sound a bit dismal.
Flapjack the morning into something bitter-
sweet
gratefulness to see this
persistence for light.
Do I have a negativity bias
towards transformation?
Weathering hate
and dancing
in this spectacular windfall
takes some chances
or some charring.
It's downright oracular
wanting incipience *here*.
Hopefully gallivanting
through phenomenal territory
while trailing my own
individual backlash
for something better.
Assuaging encounters with the past
a pitted
stomach-ing wander-
lust
and the all-too familiar
reaction to disappear
into an amorphous tide
and forget my own
name.

A SUBURBANITE TURNED RURALITE

Stabilize me
in the four walls
of my childhood home.
Trove of pictures
of younger me
and the quintessential quagmires
I found myself in.
The end of my twenties is
forming nearby
in the next frame.
I am my own idea of madness—
flatlining like unleavened bread,
or maybe
black-and-white photos.
Those cul-de-sac cavalier days
on Twelve Pines Dr.
Remembering nowadays,
without apprehension
the coincidences of that place
far gone.
Now,
furnishing a future
in far off lands
against all predictions
she's a suburbanite turned ruralite.

MEASURING THE INTENSITY OF LIGHT

A magnifying glass
to an ant's anterior.
Narrow the sun into
a last-moment laser beam.
the first taste of sidewalk power—
just cul-de-sac kids
measuring the intensity of light.

NEXT DESTINATION

Farewell is such a rushed goodbye.
Too soon.
Departing, departing.

WHITE MARE

Blank stares
and white mares
across desert-scapes.
Only time will tell
I wish you well
as I ride off into daybreak.

ROLLING STONE

A girl from the southwest
raised on a rolling-stone road.
Tongue out,
hot lips licking the steering wheel
following the direction of sanded arrowheads.

CRACKHEAD CLIMBERS

To the crackhead climbers of Indian Creek:
The gravity fighters.
The self-discovery disciples.
The desert dirtbags.
Solving hand-hold riddles through craggy covenants,
getting sandy and send-y
making sacrificial homages
of chapped, calloused, and bloody hands strewn with gobies—
a well-accepted fate.
No delayed belays
just chalked-out crevices.
Beta-analyzing
on nook-and-cranny nimbleness.
Upward
in an any-way-you-can manner.
They're holding on:
body-to-arm-to-hand-to-finger-to-rock
to grip sanity sane-less.
They're a little wild, yes.
But in this sandstone solace
their reverence is paid
in sunbaked scaled ascensions
southwestern sunsets
and right-side-up rallying.
These sacred landscapes
are for relishing bittersweet red-rock reunions.
A privilege, a pride,
a place of cathartic clutching.
Come both novice and neurotic.
Come experience the desert magic.
A place where
we climb
we climb
climb on.

DANCING WITH STRANGERS IN LOS SANTOS

Stratifying skin layered up like lust
Moon movement, rotational force
Room's a-spinning, take the lead
Hips tectonic, hand primer
West-coast flinging
Waisted (wasted) decisions
Mood-to-music, heart beat-bopping
Top 40 trance
Hi, I go by Lance.
Buzzed and baked
Low and slow, crockpot style
Cloaked in the cross fade
Quite the charmer
Blurred bodies, boding well
Here for the night
Hit replay
Dressed for a disco
Diva-dreaming
Reverberating repercussions
Of the emboldened bass
Volume up
We're going down, degenerately
Knees, ninety-degrees, nearly there
Misbehave in front of the bartender
Funked-up flirt
Groovy gal
Pirouette midnight on the hem of my dress
Drown out the crowd
Cheers!
Another round
Call me to center stage
Dip me in the Dougie
Dancing with strangers in Los Santos.

DANCE FLOOR DRUNKEN DELINQUENTS

merciless hand grabbers of the dance floor
acting before asking
violators in more ways than one.
consent was never discontinued
as if it were going out of style.

DESERT DEVOTION

Yucca moths pollinate Joshua trees
A habitat of little rain
Wind-blown tumbleweeds
In the desert we remain.

Prickly-pear pinks
Indian paintbrush-ed buttes
Strata-ed out sandstone
The place of the Paiutes.

Arroyos and aridity
We're off on a blessed quest,
It's a lifelong love affair
With the American Southwest.

LAKE POWELL

Then, my sister and I mourned fish carcasses
in beach-bowed ceremony.
Rock-and-pebble gravesites
grieving, too, my father's desertion.
Caked in mud, castles of sand
Wonder Bread sandwich crusts for looming loons
and carbohydrate-craving carp.
(All before white bread wildlife feeding wasn't frowned upon
of course).
Tube-launched Icarus's,
Life-vested to the sun before gravity's gargantuan belly flop.
Youth:
Dad-deprived, but not of dirt.
Now, the lake stratifies a drought,
fatherless for a decade.
Arid pastimes, an arrowhead lost in sand's timeclock
thunderstorm's mighty sob is holding out
flash-flood reminiscence.
Night's lightning streak sparks a memory
but recollection's reserves are running dry.
On the news broadcast, I hear the desert is evaporating—
sandstone strata reveal what once was.
A polaroid comparison:
A current spring-break picture at Lone Rock
to an old cheeky childhood aqua-socked smile.
The former:
thirsting for the latter's now-languished liquid.
A spatial disappearance like vanishing paternity.

Like Lake Powell,
I know not if I am
full
or empty
or something in between.

VENTURER

My vagabond visions
are too restless to rally in routine.
Let me saunter into magnolia sunsets
dig in the spurs of my frontier boots
and strut to a scratched Bob Dylan record—
authentically and unabashedly
just waiting for the world to catch up.

THE PRESERVATION OF OUR STORIES

I always had a knack for writing stories in the sand.
Stranded driftwood storyteller,
washed-away articulations
playing in the wake of rippled time travel.
An arrowhead-searcher
glimpsing hieroglyphic marks connecting two epochs:
an intersecting tale of
past and present—
red-tainted clay on Navajo sandstone.
I, too, collect my own anecdotes
for jest
or for preservation
wishing that my words
will withstand eras
not yet here
and never, never
wash away.

BEARS EARS

Shrinking southwestern national monuments:
a result of a presidency's betrayal.
Heard he had a distaste for Desert Solitaire.
So, I pay a homage to Abbey
grab a monkey wrench
and a gang of peaceful vigilancees.
In true environmental rebellion
I name my first-born son
Hayduke.

OPEN ROAD

Homesick for nowhere
in particular. Perhaps
just an open road.

RAMBLER REQUIEM

Rambling souls never return
the unsung pleasantries
of arctic warblers—
transplant reciprocation
is an unrequited act.
Dabbling in twilight's immersion
doting upon the thickets
of stubble and tiered flannels
toward tongue topography transgressions.
State-to-state clean slates
and new mates
Praise be the monarchs' martyrdom travel!
All hail the harmonica hum!
We're floating in the hallucinogenic hour
with high-arched bare feet
strolling on undecipherable maps
fledging to be more forthcoming
with each enlivening adventure.

ON THE ROAD

Never trust an on-the-road Jack Keroac.
Discombobulated bobblehead on the dash,
a breaking point of kerosene.
Jinxing myself on purpose
meshing well with the Beat Generation—
a lack of intrinsic importance
or social construct?
I've got something to say
(at least for now)
pondering, per usual:
Do our nodes bode well for intersection
or are we just meant for deviation?
These high
and byways:
linkages to another lover
across boundaries
I forget to make
time
and time
again.

TAMA,RISK

The barometer reads:
Infatuations with thunder's whipsaw—
there's pressure to turn back.
Sky's jarring *crack*!
Strikes the horizon in a desert blackout.
What risk do you take to see the light?
A white jagged edge
in a FLASH—
flood.
Washout zones in tragic turbidity.
Slot canyons subject to mercurial flows
a higher-ground hunkering down
measure erasure with newly deposited sand.
Tamarisk invades youthful infatuations
with unbeknownst peril.

ORION'S BELT

I'm in the thrust of a nebulous narrative
and in desperate need of hardening—
Even Mercury is running for its money this retrograde.
Lip-to-lip with lunar's one giant leap for
woman, kindly
imprinting a dream I once had
of two lover's midnight flesh heap
and spring's sweet equinox-al climax.
Hyper-fixated on indulgence and sego lily resilience
ratcheting me back to the dis-alignment of
falling | failing
stars | starts.
The sun,
misshapen in its hungry ferocity
luring attention back
into mirage's fascination
for false magic.
Branded backsides on even the most
free-ranging of cosmic cattle
orbiting new pastures
and rustling with a recon mission
that's in final surrender
to sunset's hue-ing cue.
Curious luminosity peers over
summit's straight-edged silhouette:
I satiate the darkness
with dripping candlelight
and strip down
from the clingy tendencies of fabric.
With the remainder of the day's piping exhaust,
Earth gives its wild endorsement
as I bore into reckless abandon
and take off
Orion's belt.

GOOD VIBES ONLY

Crested butte and purpureal hues
we are roseate on the red rock.
A mellow encounter
good-vibe empower-er
in whereabouts unknown.
In a double-deuced peace sign
see you soon
you say,
which will never be soon enough.

HALF-TAMED BRONCO

He's a Chris Stapleton *Sweet Symphony* song
apartment roller-blading bandit
a mullet-ed, well-mannered man,
twirling a two-step cougar
in an opportune west-coast swing occurrence.
Quoting the Outfield, he
likes his girls a little bit older.
Perusing each other's prose,
this predestined pillow talk is getting poetic
of the wistful wonder years that lie ahead
and, although the paths from Warroad
led a half-tamed, harmonica-bending bronco
to the City of Salt,
Alaska remains
in the back pocket of his midwestern mind.

STALE GRAHAM CRACKERS

For a while,
I was getting by on stale graham crackers.
Barricaded drug-house doors and boil-water notices.
Not tattle-telling on my next-door neighbor
who got a puppy
in a no-pets apartment.
Mosquito hitched a joyride
on my sunburn.
Townies shocked I moved to Alaska
alone.
Must be running from something.
They're not wrong.
In the private confines of this 300-square feet
a fleet of bathroom-mirror affirmations:
Your beautiful life is an inspiration to so many.
Be free.
Another distressed roadside penny
in the mason-jar piggy bank.
Times are flying by,
and I'm scraping up all I've got just to live this dream.

CREDENCE TO ALASKAN WINDS

converging with the city of her upbringing,

she christens this homesickness.

the far distant past is a peculiar attraction

that she flocks,

hellaciously,

away from.

turning,

in self-reinvention,

from the shackles of salt lake.

in a quarter-inch belief

in herself,

she lends credence to

alaskan winds

for anchorage.

GOOD RIDDANCE

Journeywoman wordsmith
flighty aspirations
head-in-the-clouds thinking
of alternative primed paths
past points-of-no-return periods—
I always have a hard time understanding endings.

Bliss touched me once,
just happened to be when I was writing about running away.
Now that I've ran away
I'm waiting for Bliss to catch up . . .

But I think she's being timid
and stuck in the palmed past.

When she finally arrives,
she'll chase down tales in XTRATUF strides—
and if there's one thing I know:
good riddance looks good on her.

FATE HAS FREE SHIPPING

It's me being a bit uninspired.
Undaunted by spend-thrift theories
of what-the-fuck-am-I-doing?
Universe forcing my hand
and delivering fate to my doorstep
(with free shipping)—
saying:
No charge if you take the first step.
But this recluse has no clue
a pawn in my own board-game indecision.
I am asymmetrical
(at the moment)—
mystery-solving,
glasses in magnified proportion.

How the self-discoverable deed
ultimately transpired
goes as such:
In bush Alaska
with a G2 5mm extra fine-point black-inked pen
by my own damn self
rewriting the rules to that which is unfinished.

FURTHER WEST

My friend asks:
How much further west can you go?
I say:
I'll go as far as circumnavigating the globe
just to end up right back here in Alaska
in places so remote
where I can finally hear
the sound of
my own
voice.

TREE RINGS

a two-hour upper-thigh tattoo
tree-ring limb,
demarcating twenty-eight
years on this roundabout Earth
a symbol how grounding
these longevity legs are able
to take root
but also
have the strength
to walk away.

IN MY STEVIE NICKS BANGS ERA

In my Stevie Nicks bangs era
new-Toyota-truck-Buckaroo-in-Barcelona-red era
milky-quartz-crystal-wearing-hippie-girl-self-healing-good-aura era
stained-glass-admirer-but-not-at-church era
$400-Kitchen-Aid-purhcase-to-bake-a-cheesecake-for-my-lover era
remembering-to-charge-my-vibrator era
becoming-my-own-best-friend era
not-afraid-to-make-the-first-move era
two-stepping-until-2 a.m. era
dancing-in-the-kitchen era
dancing-anywhere-when-I-feel-like-it era
self-publishing-my-second-book era
giving-my-voice-to-the-world-unabashedly era
leaning-into-my-true-self era. . .

and liking it.

ERA POEM, REVISITED.

Let my bangs yield to an era I wish I was born into, chasing down Stevie Nicks lyrics in my new Toyota Tacoma truck. Less toeing-the-line and more towing-people-out energy. Leaning into the power-red phase because all I've ever really been was a cool blue sensitive sensation, calm-cucumber appeaser. Getting-comfortable-being-uncomfortable era—guess I'm in the thick of it. Dangling amethyst on necked silver chain, my intuition is speaking up now. Chrystal-quartz healer, chakra-enhancing. A patron of stained-glass art, the charming kind with no religious undertones. Spontaneously purchasing a baby blue Kitchen Aid mixer, justifying it with *it'll last me a lifetime* logic, when lord knows I just want to make a cheesecake for a *chef's kiss.* Always-charged-*electronics* is a sign of single-woman adulting. Dust-kickin' in my yeehaw boots, two-steppin' into my own damn heart—call it falling in love. My voice articulated in a self-published paperbacked book. *Shucks! Did I just make myself proud?* I'm not one for lengthy introductions, but I'm Lancee, and I kind of like that . . . finally.

WANTED, AS IF FOR RANSOM

There's a time differential between
tomorrow and the six of swords.
In five years,
ask me if I am still staring down conformity or
covering up domestic abuse's cigarette-butt burn
like branded cattle.

Cage me not.
wings diverting away from custom of the female *sorry*.
Every act I do without confidence
is a male opportunist's way to pretend it was his
sprung-out-of-nowhere idea.

Of all the names I do answer to
it will never be
yours.

So, I lower my toes into another lukewarm lover.
He states:
Tell me how you want to be wanted.

I reply:
Wanted,
as if for ransom.

SUMMER

Bear
Deterrent

GOOD MORNING

bacon-grease perfume
yoking the dawn
into a splatter
paint of
sunny-side up
starts.

THE UNBLEMISHED MAGIC OF IRRESPONSIBILITY

If you so dare:
Strip down under candle glow
and run through midnight grass
with red-wine veins—
singing tunes of the unforgotten dog days.
Riverbank teens
and runaway queens
the moment is lived in the here and now
or we shall be banished to adulthood.

We feel profound through firsts
smiling in a sacrosanct summer
cherishing the unblemished magic
of irresponsibility
that ends when our parents
call out:
Come home.
Wondering,
when we will just
grow up.

SUN CHASER

Sun chaser, infuse.
Indulge the long-awaited
light

beaming from above.

WAYFARER SKIES

amalgamation of clouds

day-drifting

wafting

in a wayfarer manner

in

an open

sea

of western

sky.

CUMULUS

It's a boat!
It's a shark!
It's a fish!
It's a collective cloud pastime.
(Or micro-dose's apparition).
An atmospheric metamorphosis
right before your eyes
skyline sublime
or even a

       lofty

            cumulus

                 ~transcendence~

DEAR DEMING

A bare-cheeked greenhouse ordination.
Memories of Moon Valley
cross my mind's clearing
years later, I think of you fondly.
In that affinity for fresh air
I recall the blooms came late that sanguine season
but were surely just as beautiful.
Scattershot hair
wind-whipping my rosy cheeks
jovial dancing in sunflower-strewn fields
toes laced with girthy-wormed dirt
a voice, dandy—full of promise
a bluegrass band in empty silo sessions
a peachy, wild-horse-pastured peacekeeper
savior from the crazed chicken-coop turkey
discoverer of behind-the-barn-door eggs
spoon-carver of white-pined projects
expert weeder of strawberry-patched hearts
best bolo-tied biker of Nooksack backroads.
It's a water-tank cannonball—

SPLASH!

Cinderella pumpkins and first-kiss melons
a North Cascades creed
a simple night
a simple town
living the simple life.
I hung to the tractor's cliffside, carefree
one hand, braced to the metal frame
the other, raised invincibly
as we headed due west for sunset.
To my dear Deming friend:
With all gratitude within my soul
you are love and light
and always will be.

VALLEY OF THE MOON

Take me to calendula-filled caresses
lemon balm baths
and to brimming bluegrass bands.
To spearmint stuck smiles
and soul-enriching soils
mesmerizing milkweed moments
and monarch butterfly mysteries.
Take me to picturesque plantain potlucks
to bee hums and hive havens
and to the Pacific's welcoming waters.
Take me to horsetail happiness
hummingbird harmonies
nestling nettle
and to Nooksack river naps.
To behold borage's beauty
and to be comforted by comfrey.
Take me to reinvigorating rays
lemon-verbena vibes
and chamomile's calming effects—
take me to the valley of the moon.

SIN CITY

Blue Moon beers
in five-star hotels
scrabble *jackpot*
gamble with staying in tonight.
Vegas stripped us
as we folded into a California king.
Cut my edge,
call it beginner's luck
lottery-flashed smile
winner winner
take-home buffalo-chicken-pizza dinner.
According to the well-known theory
what happens in this place must stay here
and so must this one night shared.
But we learn an empty-pocket lesson:
Fortune isn't just casino-made
and even in Sin City
you can be saved.

DIRECTION IS AN ILLUSION

The sun skinny dips into the horizon—
I always found it to be a little risqué
to flirt with golden hour.
Cornfield runner
pathway illuminated by firefly grace,
at this time of night
humidity clings
to every midwestern sweat droplet.
On the cusp of a contra dance in Minnesota
on my way to nowhere
minding my own manners
on the interstate—
call me a road sage.
Milling about like scattered wind
pining for juniper
and Pacific summers.
Where am I running from?
Or where am I headed towards?
Direction never seems
to be quite linear.
Truth North is not
an internal compass
and may actually be
taking me
West.

MOUNTAIN MORNING

This West Coast sermon
idolizing our life in an alpenglow aura.
Dear,
have you awakened yet
from your Sierra sarcophagus?
The sun's been pining for you lately.
She's coming up now
navigating us toward ascension.
Hurry up!
We're being summoned to summit.

HITCHHIKING 101

You're shit outta luck (and gasoline).
Free-spirit flower child,
your riveting cross-country ride
through aspens, alders, pine
is on a temporary

Pause.

Lust for northern latitudes
love for western longitudes
is roadside.
Note: There is an art of decorum to hitch-hiking.
Wrangle up courage
thumb-out debutante
ask only in the daylight.
Drink water you dehydrated damsel-in-distress
iodine purification tablets in a stream-dunked Nalgene.
Concealed carry with class
even if it is just bear spray
share your location with the geographically closest friend
better have that phone charged
send a photo of the vehicle
include the make, model, and description of the driver.
And when you think back to when mama said:
Never get in the car with a stranger
remember,
while danger looms at every crossroad
calculated risk exists in each leg of the journey.
You get in anyway
and *click* the seatbelt
just to be safe.

DEWY

Dew drops from white-pine needles
incandescently adhering to the properties of water.
A bended-light glistening
holding molecules by the thousands
refracting delight.

CONSTELLATION CONSPIRING

Afterglow spectating
The stars: an illustration immaculate.
Eyes on those wayward sparkles
conspiring in constellation contours.
No words uttered in awe—
wonder repeated verbatim.

NIGHT, EVERLASTING

Under beaming blankets of stars
we gaze at cosmos above
then at each other.
Wishing for an everlasting night
I was a dancing-on-air kind of happy—
a perfect state of being.
Plotting the sky
us, uncharted.

OUTER SPACE EXISTENTIAL CRISIS

Black holes and burning stars
smell like existential decay.
I scream into the void
dilapidated universe.
Time and space are of no importance.

ISLAND ISOLATION

Three months of summer
never went by so slow
when each day you dream of dying
on the island of alone.

ROCHE HARBOR (SORT-OF) SUGAR MAMA

The next-door neighbor's llama greets me
as I bike down the lane
in blueberry-stained jeans
to the farm's bunkhouse.

Stretching the outer limits of a wish,
I petitioned to get on a sugar daddy's luxury 90-foot yacht
that summer.
But manifestation made sugar taste like femininity.
I met a sugar *mama* with *daddy's* money.
Close enough, right?
The universe has a salt-water taffy sense-of-humor.

Sugar gave me a posh $7 sprinkle-topped donut
and I discarded harsh preconceptions
about hoity-toity ocean-harbor wealth.

In Fourth of July's heat
Andromeda dotted the sky in sparkler lures.
We were crab-leg canoodle-ing
log-spinning lovers
bottle-rocket kisses exploding
like a thousand opium poppies
high as a cricket's shrill cull.

Like departing morning dew—
fair but fleeting—
that water limousine left me
in a white-capping wave catharsis.

Still tasting sugar on my lips
I learned why boats are always named after women.

HORIZON'S HAMLET

A sunset departure.
Here comes an onset
of seeping-in balmy blue tones
with an albatross ascension
in the foreground.
Filter in now
laughs, legend, lore
as congregations round crackling logs
toes rummage through sifted sand.
Cradled in sunlight's remainder,
today falters on the horizon.

HUMMINGBIRD

You can have my heart
when you hold it like a hummingbird.

Quench me in sugar water
and let me hum vibrato.

Meet me in Mexico next season?

ON THE COAST OF SOMEWHERE BEAUTIFUL

Madrona-tree isles hold me in their matriarchal care.
The full moon murmurs its tidal secrets
as I succumb to the guidance of lighthouses
especially in my darkest hour.
In winged deliverance,
I emulate the eagle
and showcase the wings I wish I possessed
in feathered weightlessness—
it's my turn to take flight
I am ready
to listen to the prophecy of orca's warrior song
and the hallowed messages of humpback's hailing in—
this San Juan serendipity just might save me.
I forget to check the time
dive into a lily-pad strewn lake
tend to the coop, crack jokes
but not the eggs!
Greet the flock with a:
What's up chicken butt!?
I braid strands of rainbow into my hair each morning
and become my own pot of gold.
I protect what I love,
this island,
giving myself permission to do the same with my heart.
I take a dandelion in this unsure hand
and with a bellowing breath
I make a

                        W   S
                            I

                                                    H

BULL KELP AND OTHER TREASURES

The fast-growing bull kelp
that once steadfastly gripped the ocean floor
now washed onto beaches by the rough-and-tumbling Pacific.
Alien-like and slimy
seaweed lines the pebbled sand.

Clay
earthen mud
ceramic class on my face
a naturalist day spa.

Sea-shell ears
I hear my calling echoed by the ocean's lull
I am unsure if I'm ready to listen.
A concerto of cymbal tides
Crash
Crash
Crash
the current makes demands on me.

Petrified tree
driftwood dreaming
washed up past the high-water mark.
A beached bench
for my bottom.

Sea glass, glimmering
the curvature of eroded sharpness.
Pure speculation:
Perhaps the discards of drunkard pirates ages past
or other stories we dare conjure—
the origins of things left behind.

A footprint
fleeting.
There
a wave
the culprit
for the disappearance
of sole's brief imprint.

Skipping stone
quick-stepping gravity's defiance.
Succumbing to a plunge
the centuries old tendency to play
and play we must make ritual.

Simple discoveries
the abundance of sea trinkets
rests assuredly
ashore.

DREAMSCAPE TOMORROW

Wellness checks and rainbow reminders
pick me up,
country-dance style.
Life elevated
forever ingrained
in our Sandy (Utahan) souls
but no longer our final resting place.
We reckon
it's *always* mountain time.
Nostalgia remembers you fondly
as we discover
that the home we've yearned for
has been holding our hands
all along.
Abiding by the no-sad-songs-in-the-car rule
and hair in unbridled curls
western winds teach us
it's ok to fly
with our gently repaired wings
and dreamscape tomorrow
as if it's the last thing
we have to hold on to.

FLAME'S RESISTANCE

Smokejumper in urgent flight
over ignited western brush.
Breath in rapid resuscitation,
raspy
dried-out mouth
gasping in crackling air
conducting carbon-controlled burns.

The forest is flammable,
let-it-burn landscape—
there's an onset
of a stratospheric stressor
estimating the smoldering acreage,
ravaged by char
environmental attributes
in ember red.

Manage risk
moisture extinction
evaporating in singed *sayonara*
a vast ton of propagating particulate
in an ashed-out sky
blaze in convective complication rampage.

A precursor to coal
advancing inferno intake
dangerous reliance on heat.

Scorched sweat
in a flaring gold-streaked sky
ceasing energy
in unending fire,
he finally puts an end
to flame's resistance.

JUMP INTO THE LAKE

An intended seasonal sacrifice
dismantling my core.
Bedroom-dancing with chaos
skinny-dipping with sin
afloat by dishonesty
I am in the wake
of my own mistakes.
Riesling drips
down a delicate moment
onto rain-pattered cabin
temporarily liberated by libations.
Photos cradling destined encounters
of two (e)strangers.
Admonished by a tear
bludgeoned by a tongue
vacated a vacation
in vacillating flight.
Lost in intangible promises
I write a poem where I call you *lover*
and within a year's time,
I forget your name
completely.

FORGIVENESS OF A WANDERING FOOL

Have a shot of whiskey with my shadow
Two-step with my ghost
There's a million people in this world,
But you're the one I wanted most.

When I leave this coastal town,
Will you still think of me?
Still bearing my last name
Reckoning a broken family tree.

While my journey begins anew
Your face is framed in the overlook
I'm off to distant lands
Our story penned in a drifter's sunken book.

I'll travel to god-only-knows where
Please remember me in the good light
Sea side in that village harbor
As the salmon run, surely so must I.

Now chasing my wildest dreams
Cherishing that heart-stopping view of the bay,
Softened by left-side-of-the-bed memories
By your body I once laid.

Still pining for you and for that place
What ifs can be so mighty cruel,
Now what if I came back asking
For the forgiveness of a wandering fool?

SALMON SEASON SEMI-HAIKU SERIES

Seagull, far above.
I shit you not, shorebird sky
shat atop my head.

Sun-dripped white-cap wait.
Wing-spree eagle flies high up.
Tide, sneaks closer, to me.

Anadromous fish.
Migrate. Meander. Move.
Headed home. To die.

Alevin, a new hatch.
Eventually to sea.
Come back soon. Bigger.

Skipper and greenhorn.
First season out at high sea.
Tension. Tides. Teaching.

Salmon wrangler wrestle.
Net-mender mentality:
Cork, lead, line, float, sink.

XTRATUF, Grundens.
Blood, slime, and scale-covered suits.
Rubber-brands of Bristol Bay.

Salmon June junkies.
Gillnet, seine, troll, net the depths.
Red-fever season.

Boat in hot pursuit.
Slamming salmon, heavy-net hunk.
Bleed gill, next one.

Bird, bear, buyer—splash.
Fish hits deck. Fast. Future feast.
Everyone hungers.

Wake-drawn lines, buoyed.
Eager. Entrap. Escapement.
An eye of the sock.

Mud-spattered waders,
Largest salmon run, sprinting.
Frenzied fishing folk.

Fish assembly line.
Filet, vacuum seal, labeled.
A freezer-bound bounty.

Fish filet. Salt-brined.
Soak, drain, dry. Smoked out, slowly.
Dock delicacy.

Gales, gut checks, grime glow.
A neoprene nostalgia.
A sea-sick serene.

Puke, piss in bucket.
Off the rocker or rails, purge.
Pill pop, ocean stomach.

Fishing subsistence.
Catch a count. Release excess.
Share. The Salmon Way.

MOTIVES TO SET SAIL

In the non-existence of June's darkness
the boat wharf illuminated
by powerful float-dock flashlights.
He navigates the fore cabin
his domain of dereliction.
Anchored to a gale-prone girl
embanked on an archival
of her poetry
wondering
why he harbors a heart
snagged on a castaway catastrophe
collapsing like this year's salmon fishery.
Ready to cast lines
toward secluded scales
a sockeye savior
Johnny Cash skipper
fleeing the summer
like an over-fished fugitive
singing *Folsom Prison Blues*
from the stern
roving a beam
of his last-hope smile
to shore
missing her
mending her
motives to set sail.
A somber goodbye
from sand
to the safety
of the sea's
solicitude.

FELDSPAR

Trembling voice, sliding fret fingers
Music to my ears
Hoping he's not scared or ravaged
By all my darkest fears.

These shadows burn like whiskey
And smoothly so does he
Bedsheets put to rest
The fondest of our friendly memories.

Lapping the shore
Of my own derelict daydreams
Falling into his ocean
Of lustful sultry schemes.

Am I living for the moment?
Or am I living for the larks?
Hunkering down
Needing nape nests and armistice arms.

Closing curtains
On his devil haloed charm
Ecstasy abounds in his eyes
Glints of all-consuming feldspar.

Sanity wavers in uncertainty
Running to his savior's ship
In the safety of misbehavior's
Sultry smitten lips.

On the verge of my verse's
Craving aching storm
Like thunder and lightning
Elements of nature forlorn.

Our breath is backed
By candle's lighted wick
These chords articulating the laws
Of two lovers transfixed.

MAKE ME WATER

Be it attraction
or something tethered.
Just synapses and breath
two souls amongst the
density of a bedroom
but yet I know,
when we are well
within our circumferences
you feel the tension, too
touching the surface
needingly, but need not
say any fathomed word
or say anything, really
at all.

COBALT'S REASSURANCE

In a land far far away
we find ourselves
in the labyrinthine ebbing tide.
The moon guides us
in safe transit
as we are chilled
in oceanic breeze.
The past,
recedes into the background
and we are astonished
by admiralty antics.
Sentimental over a village harbor
sleepless in aquatic blue
we, as loons,
swoon over sapphire hour
so becoming
at this time of night.
High on a coastal rush
the sea is our sage
as we channel a
continually changing course
in cobalt's reassurance.

SUMMER SOLSTICE

And somehow,
the days turned into summer
peaking in heat, prematurely
a solstice arrival.
The jet boat:
On step with our journey
skimming the surface of
our greatest potential—
an SPF 50, no-sunburn zone
zinc in constant reapplication.
Cedar-tree smellers
mosquito-bite scratchers
and spaghetti-western watchers
of projected films
reeling on the side
of red-dusted,
wood-paneled,
hay-infused barns.
Outdoor kitchen aficionados
sprinkling M&M's on popcorn
in the collective cooking spirit
camaraderie-like
perfecting the sweet-to-salty ratio.
Unfolding passed-down lawn chairs.
In those unforgettable dog days—
we are dandelion holders
wishing
wishing
that these moments
never dissipate.

LUSTING AFTER RAINBOWS

It's a fly line, leader, tippet: A trance.
Chartreuse, a word, just-learned
color-schematic lures
lusting after rainbows.

BEAR TRACKS

A fresh mud-imprinted halt
a risk not-worth-taking
a bear-tracks turnaround.
Trying to get the heck-outta-Dodge
Durango, ditch-dwelling
we become rear-end physics finessers
atop suspended bumpers
see-saw-ing motion
to steady a veered-off-the-road vehicle.
A state-park trooper's "tug"
on Tugatuk road.
We opt out of bear country, barely.
Watercolor weekenders
brush-stroking survival's scene.
What are adventure days
but a slew of various hazards?

HOLY CRACKLE JOLLY

I sit on a grassy knoll, writing this.
Chronicling the characters in
my $11 salmonberry-covered journal.
A young blonde-haired kiddo
does a rolly-polly-olly
down the gentle gradient-ed slope
yelling *HOLY CRACKLE JOLLY!*
as he descends in an uncontrolled bodily rotation
down the green-patched hill.
I giggle and take delight in
the child's exclamation of choice—
the utmost silliness of language spewed from
young tongues
but I remember the words I make up in my own poems
how similarly odd
never-to-appear in stringent dictionaries.

A young couple
smidges up close to one another
quilted and quiet, co-mingling.
I may be eye-line imposing (or staring)
but how beautiful does their love appear to an outsider (me).
Perhaps I'll cohabitate with the emotion one day.

A widow (I surmise)
takes pleasure reading cowboy smut.
Yeehaw.
I tip my ball cap in a
dedicated manner to our irreverent selves.
Public erotica reading, a cause I can support.
Sometimes what is fantasy is better than reality, and
I think of all the poems of fictitious men I wish existed
and a spurred-out cowboy I once had the pleasure of
two-stepping with until 2 a.m. at some hometown ho-dunk saloon.

But this twenty-something era is cavalier to caring males—
better stick to bookshelf partnerships.

Ah! A people-watching afternoon well spent.
I am homebound.
In route
I spare the life of
an indecisive squirrel in a mid-road panic.
I mental note the critter's almost life-changing event
while philosophizing (without a proper degree)
what makes one successful in the prose profession.

I conclude:
Perhaps to be a *poet*
is to simply pay attention
to all things of importance
but also, to matters of inconsequence
giving voice to moments
that we frequently tend to   pass by.

REFULGENCE

The refulgence of the crescent moon
bursts into my brightest dreams—
we share starlit smiles and s'mores
hung up on hammock-forested nights.

RECESSIVE LUPINE

The lupine's gone recessive:
Blue to a pinkish/white.
Like it
we evolve
revive
into newer
and rarer
versions of ourselves.

THE UNDERTOW

You linger on these leeward lips
keeping me close
but not close enough.
I'm lost
in a flow-state fervor
in lust's luring fleet.
It's unfathomable
these handheld figure-eight-knot habits
I can't seem to break free from.
Towing the undercurrents
of your mind.

LA-DI-DA-LAUDANUM

Finding death's outlet in
a myriad of self-exiting strategies.
Altering fate's last recall
peace gives permission
that I may meet finality's
eternal rest.
A perennial spirit decides
against renewal.
The Dahlias mourn dolefully
at this.
Hear the rain's lament!
Before spring's arrival, buried in
benevolence's rosy aura, I find
veneration in sudden-departure songs:
La-di-da-laudanum.

PASTIME

My favorite pastime besides poetry
is putting my life at risk.
Been saving myself for a special occasion
(or a suicide attempt)
just not sure when that'll ever be.
Dressed to the nine lives and
nothing-else-left neck tie,
hung up on the color blue.
Depression: that disease doesn't
even want to attend the after party and
sanity must be too far-reaching
for even the closest of stars.
Time for travel, cutting my
trip around the sun a bit short
this year, so
please place me into a collapsible carry, on
a first-class flight to the funeral
and take me
far away
somewhere away from
the knife drawer
and all its *sharpened* lies.

59TH PARALLEL INHALATION

Inhale.
Been ritualizing looking up at the sky
beckoning for a belonging
aspiring to be tidal.

Exhale.
Claiming antidotes too far below the surface
into the eddies I go
swirling into oblivion.

Inhale.
Familiarizing myself with the state of p r o l o n g e d
pauses . . .
vacillating with the waves, cresting
lapping the shore, so surely—
can it mist me in its natural confidences?

Exhale.
Calm-infusion and coastal salt
brining my future's preservation.

Inhale.
Resurface.
Resurface.
Resurface that breath held in the depths of laboring lugging lungs.

Exhale.
Drowning out dark testimonies I once subscribed to
sinking, now, with the Pacific's permission.

Inhale.
Soul settling into the 59th parallel
reclaiming land's stabilization
surviving the sea's synapses, firing.

Inhale again.
Embracing my longing-for-lighthouses
a finding-my-way flickering
then coming back into this world in a flash
slowly.

Exhale.

MINDFULNESS

Regenerative retreat to the mountains
quiets the day's frenzy
and overactive mind—
amassing a never-ending duration
of wonder
mesmerizes me every time.

JUST STAY

it was never my forte to
just stay.
that is
until I found a place
where I simply
could not
move on from
anymore.

SILENCING SHOT

Singe of his gun-hot hands
hasty to the touch.
Deja-vu days
reliving our pasts primal instincts.
Sweat-backed memories
relapsing in the heat of it all
sweltering.
There's an art to building anticipation—
tasting sweet birch-water elixirs
and carving inscriptions
of two lovers' tree-barked initials
barreling down a dirt road
revolving in these deep-rooted fears
that I'll never write a piece
as poignant as the last
or that you'll decide to leave
without trigger-warning.
Today's our tempting teacher
sight fixated on my chest—
adrenaline antidote
action-ready.
I'm in the line of heart's fire
facing my last silencing shot.

COWBOY HAIKUS

Ho-dunk bar *howdy*.
Tip-of-the-hat two-stepper.
Sir Whiskey Wallen.

His generous pour
on the rocks. Kentucky smooth.
She's one-hundred proof.

RED LIGHT, GREEN LIGHT

Green light: *Go*. But I'm in a Ford Bronco, gut-wrenched and gas-pedal hesitant. A mile out of town, barely cresting city limits. *Ride the Lightning – 717 Tapes* by Warren Zeiders acoustic in my ears, the soundtrack to every cowboy archetype I've ever chased, brandishing steel instead of softness, never-to-be-tamed roughstocks, red-necking my heart tame.

Red light: *Stop*. And I'm back in a Stetson stalemate—the revving gets me nowhere closer to a revival. Bucking the clutch in a breakaway from the throes of death's final *yeehaw*.

Green light: Go. Close my eyes, riding the middle line, wavering between the law and letting go, hair sprawled gravity-less in downed window's wind tunnel, sundress seeking midnight's promising *Pretty Little Poison.*

Green light: GO. Straight through crossroad's chute and back to wrangling the neon moon. A stranger's foreign two-step, taming a bar bull's mechanics, thigh bruised. High West bourbon straight from the saloon's pearl-snap suitors, bolo-tie banter with knockin' boot intentions.

Red light: *STOP*. Languishing in his laughter, lassoing me right back to the clutch of a cactus. Tethering me to brassey belt buckles and his temperamental beard-branded stallion on my neck, nights of barebacked bedsheet rodeos and broken promises. There's no more truth in turquoise.

Red light: Rein it in.
Red light: Risk it all?
Yellow light: Re-ride.
Yellow light: Saddle up.
Yellow light: His nocturnal nod.
Green light: Give it all you got.
Green light: Give him hell.
Red light: Give him anything but you.

TRANQUIL TRANSITIONS

The night ladles me whole
and spills me over into sunrise.

FALL

WHISKEY

THE INFANCY OF FALL

Spruce-tipped September clings
to fleeting things
and like an upturned autumnal leaf
we're in the infancy of fall.
There's a lasting possibility of perhaps
tethered to us all—
will we last this season's woolen endurance?
I have not yet loved
in long durations
yet I have loved enough
to know it's possible
to trust like the leaves
in their annual branched release,
floating earthbound
in unwary relinquish—
let my loving you be the most beautiful
d
    e
        s
            c
                e
                    n
                        s
                            i
                                o
                                    n

SEASONAL DECAY

Cloaked in my own apparition—
the spookiest thing I've yet to experience.
Fall slayed the summer
in daybreak's decrepit bludgeoning.
October demarcates darkness's steady onslaught,
and I learn about acts of cowardice
when the leaves crumble
beneath my boots,
crunch like bones—
the brittle snapping sounds
of seasonal decay.

GARDEN OF EDEN

Orchard-bitten apple
remnants of ripened rib.
Some paradise
lost.

THE LAST OF THE DAHLIAS

Yesterday
my neighbor brought me the last
of his garden's Dahlias.
With every flowered mention
flashbacks of your inked skin
enveloped in a bloom
enveloped in each other
enveloped in eternity's blanketed warmth.
Oftentimes, now
I feel myself searching for the same magic
in the mornings I meander through alone.
Begging the sunrise,
that you're seeing it today, too
and thanking the sunset that you were there, in spirit.
When the wind wisps my brunette behind my ear
breathing rescue's resin into my body
telling me still-ocean sweet nothings
I trust that our paths crossed
from more than mere happenstance.

Today
when the Dahlia bloomed with the dawn
a palpable yearning arrived
wanting to stay for fall's sacred leaf-scattering.
I manifested made-up memories again:
your mug-held hand
full of honey-infused chaga tea teeth
leading me back into the light
dancing my soul smitten.
I go on imaginatively reminiscing
until the afternoon
blaming you for loving these moments
plaguing me in nostalgia's saccharine song.

BOUNTIFUL

The harvest moon is out
and has brought me all that I have been asking for.

SALMONBERRY JAM

We revel in the salmonberry harvest
brimming over woven birch baskets.

A bounty in my hands
but I am unsure how to behold it.

It is uncanny how the world provides
subsisting
surviving
sharing.
I call this Curyung fate
to be here
yet again
alive and in good health.
It is destiny that
I have arrived
and gathered
gifts of the land
where the clean and muddy waters meet.
Finally realizing that
so much of me
is still worth
preserving.

I am something more or less shelf stable now.

ENTRAPMENT

Savage or savant?
There's something epic
about an epicurean palette
indulging on the sweet aftermath
of past fawning.
Frothing at the mouth
for a delectable future—
is it time to eat?
There's a pang in my chest,
aching for eternity
takes a hearty appetite
rapidly rabid
for a male relapse
of some sort
looking for lips
to gently sink
these incisors upon
a meal ever-so tender
sliding right off the bone
a huntress
on the prowl for
love,
a fowl and furtive creature
that hesitates to hibernate—
call it a final-course entrapment.
I set the table for one
and let him serve a means
to a bittersweet end.

FREAK ACCIDENT

A professional hockey player
gets cut in the neck by a skate
during puck time.
A baggage handler
ingested into a plane's turbine.
A child,
wrapped up in tetherball string.
Last week,
my friend's dad
slipped on some ice
and hit his head
just a little wrong
but in just the right way
to be termed a *freak accident*
so that his life
was cut shor-
t.

As I go through each day
I try to cherish
every
second
because I know
that if there are
a thousand ways to die
I have to believe
there are more
than a million ways
to live.

GRAY HAIR

The self-discovery of gray hair changes everything.
A realization of youth yielding to finiteness
dissipating by the second.
If I am of matter,
like this Earth,
then I, too, am created and destroyed
in each decaying moment
evaporating to a higher calling
transpiring for tall tales
of my transgressions
precipitating pitfalls
into water-bounty eyes—
becoming porous.
We are abridgments
of a larger narrative—
the sun's showcasing our
best wrinkled-skin smiles.
Time:
measured by the tides
moon phases
seasonal outbursts
to be documented
with this ink
I become the creator's humble archivist
holding the pen-
ultimate encounter with age.
Not the last
not quite there,
at the end,
but noticing
that I must continue to believe
that today is still so young
like me
even just at heart.

FADING FIREWEED

The fireweed burns away:
We're both in states of decomposition.

TENDER RECKONING

The South
where I go into fantasy.
Intuition: a great salesman
takes me there in bandeau lace
wire-wrapped stones—
descendance around my neck
a place of exposure
to your tender reckoning.
The truth between us
is less than forthright
a shiver stalemate
breath into fog
don't evade something as fervid, as this.
Admit desire
under the guise of Syrah burgundy
Is this night as dire
as it feels?
Vertigo and Venus,
pleasure come closer, please
a desperate condensation
we're condemned to intertwine.
Upend any state-of-being
of your once-possessed skin.
Hands are final puzzle pieces
fitted bedsheets
honey sweet
sweat
constantly making infinity
out of mole hills of Appalachia.
In the distance
are the seeds,
he planted
here.

MAYBE IT'S MABEL

Synchronization is a staple
Fill me up, ladle by ladle,
Winged hearts, maybe it's Mabel,
Fresh starts, maybe it's Mabel.

Pull out the top drawer, now,
It houses all the quipped quills
I've been drowning in an inked house
Just a damn poet, honing my lover's skill.

Synchronization is a staple
Fill me up, ladle by ladle,
Singe impart, maybe it's Mabel,
Love depart, maybe it's Mabel.

Moved to a land of abysses,
Stammering in simmered staccato kisses,
Lost in full-throttled misses,
Still stuttering from mortal killing wishes.

Synchronization is a staple
Fill me up, ladle by ladle,
Dash and dart, maybe it's Mabel,
Come apart, maybe it's Mabel.

Twirling in trebled sounds,
Stolen promises drenched and drowned
The forest sleeps, silence abounds
Calling out for a lost love ever-so loud.

Synchronization is a staple
Fill me up, ladle by ladle,
In the after dark, maybe it's Mabel,
Neither loon nor lark, maybe it's Mabel.

LIGHTNING'S SECOND STRIKE OUT

Fall, subsumed in careless atrophy
putting playlist on shuffle
because I like the unpredictability.
The rocking chair holds a steady pace,
but I'm the one off the rockers.
Ice is part delicacy part wicked edict of endings.
Pothole-dodging on a four-wheel drive to nowhere,
calling shotgun with life's misdeeds in the driver's seat.
There are no maps to mayhem (back to May) (back to him).
Only branded-skin memories
from lightning's second
strike out:
There's no home [in] running back.
Mountain musk dipped in fir scent
altered by aphrodisiac reformation, we
revel in elevated breath from whiskey's point-to-prove.
Proof that I've been a silent orator dabbling in a daydream
raspy for love's encore, a sellout, I
woke up with a tattering heart that's all
talk but never well-
rested.
It's a broken legacy of upturned boulders,
crestfallen by the insufferable recounts of
my own stolen stories.
A loose reading of Genesis
that man and woman were never made for one another.
A halo bores into my scalp
yet I keep listening to the devil's R&Blasphemy.
What an undertaking, to be human
to feel in grandiose measurements.
So, pour me a cup of expired tea and
leave me like
you mean it
this time.

HEART-SHAPED POTATO

Tire rubber runs down driveway's gravel, parks in its designated sedimental vehicular space. The grandfather-I-always-wanted neighbor greets me upon my arrival. Gratitude-filled greeting imparted as if I am back from a long and arduous journey (in this instance, my office job). My neighbor is a gardener.

The gardener asks me about my day. I ask: *What're you up to?* A cherub reply: *Oh, you know, just living in the present moment.*

The gardener is humble. Raised on circumstances of Alaska's harshness, independence became habit, yet he still provides for a community of family here in formidable landscapes. He cares for his crop, much like the world, tenderly. To strangers, like me, he offers more than I can begin to accept.

The gardener was the first man to ever give me flowers. Dahlias. Their diversity reminding me of the first man I ever loved, his tattoo-sleeved arm in delicate floral latticework. I'm overcome with reminders of universal connection, petal-sniffing my way through nostalgia, accepting the gift I've been entrusted to care for while Alaska begins to take on its first frost.

But before it sets in, the freeze, it was a Sunday. Dusk started to settle in late, his arthritic hands sifting through mounded dirt. Countless hours, unobserved by any other soul except the light, he labored. NPR on the radio, playing at the garden's outskirts. Its static jurisdiction emanating constant wavelength news. That noise: a moose-deterrent from the plot's cabbaged corners. As the hues changed their artistry, row after row after row, treasuring each Yukon Gold variety that emerged from soil's productive summer, bended knees aching, but never articulated aloud. Collecting each rounded vegetable, placing them on toboggan ride to be sledded out of the row, to be washed, sorted, bagged, then ultimately, shared. I ask to join in the gathering with him. Pleased, he welcomes my presence, as we separate each variety into baskets. Light-heartedly, he notes that he abhors discrimination of any kind, but, in the garden-context, he does like to keep the French fingerlings apart from the King Edwards.

The gardener finds a Klondike Rose heart-shaped potato, and his kind and gentle soul beams like the harvest moon symbol of bounty. *I was thinking of my granddaughter when I found this.* I take a photo of him, holding it against his flannel, radiating joy. Lines around a grizzled smile bestow me with life's acquired wisdom: *All the success in the world means nothing when there is no one to share it with. Thank you for your help tonight, I was hurting.*

The gardener reads me a poem he wrote about the time he finally got sober, and I think of my biological father—the one that walked out of my life nearly twelve (12) years ago, his alcoholic testimonies that endangered the lives of many. How the liquor tore my family apart, lured my father down a path of parting ways, into a man unrecognizable. The gardener teaches me about forgiveness, about how living in a small rural town like this, you learn to accept people for who they are, vices and all. The gardener tells of his past mistakes, his regrets, his estranged son. He speaks of the ability to overcome, to move on from pain.

The gardener wears his heart on the outside of his damp grass-stained overalls. He is great, offers me potatoes, and sends me on home for respite.

TOXIC HOROSCOPE

I remember
the way things used to be:
Clean.
Now
I drive through this place
in a little red rental car
opting for every back road
traveling,
trembling with fear
in a stain-ridden society.
Iron-soaked puddles, orange accumulating.
Getting a pedicure in pesticide polish,
I'm pretty. . .
pretty poisoned.
The fountain of our youth is
pretty polluted.
Fictional scenes of a mass EPA cleanup
dreaming of another DuPont nightmare.
For now,
I'm like the rest
making a toxic brew in the bathtub
soaking in nefariousness and nitrate.
A trickling testament of leaching iron
from my tub's sulfuric spout.
*How many of these stories
are told without recourse?*
In the afterthought of American towns
these places
subjected to
mercury's
lethal
retrograde.

FRACTAL

Welcome to the never-ending simulation fractal. Come with me on a journey around the curvature of this Blue Dot. Pyramid schemes poised in patterned triangles, uprooting the land like peaks and valleys, essential-oil vultures vying for the dying-out dollar bill. A runway model's stiletto implodes a shooting star creating dust-fragmented asphalt. It snows for the first time in the Sonoran desert, literally becoming frozen in the sands of time. Climate change just bought a red Corvette and is speeding down the interstate toward California, in her hourglass figure, running out of time, running on empty, running on rubber-burning road rage. A salmon scale, a tree ring, layers in rock, aging like the rest of us. Brick-by-brick, length times width times height, geometry-stacking shape, a craggy curmudgeon with a conical head is at home hunkering down for a hurricane. We are infinite errors mixed with finite correctness. Living in a recursive fever dream. Document the coastline in the unit of measure that you choose. Trippy applications of alliteration and we're not even on acid. Generational iterations of the same mistake. Mending my jeans/genes with Mendel. *Is our failure as intricate as we make it seem?* Bending phenomenon into conformity. I received a post-marked Hallmark card in the mail, expedited. No return address. Galaxy's last gift to me is a Y-shaped letter.

Greetings from space!
Why did the world choose destruction when it had the chance to change?
From, a fallen fractal paradox.

THE SOUTH

Before Atlanta becomes Atlantis
before New Orleans' fortification fails
before storm surges us all
to oceanic oblivion
before Dollywood drowns to *World on Fire*
on the jukebox
before Appalachia runs for the hills
before the Bayou backs down
before cypress trees go on an endangered escapade
before Baton Rouge lays down its arms
before sea bleeds out into marsh,
marches
then seeps away.

today,
a beignet at Cafe Du Monde and
I have a powdered-sugared date
with disillusionment.

TWENTY QUESTIONS

we've outgrown this earth
so let's eclipse
obscure ourselves
from the narrative
done fighting
for our species' survival
how stopgap surreal
there's more fright
than flight
these days
as we polar
freeze
frame
our world
in one last picture
say cheese
our plumage
our past
illuminates
in meteor's
showering down
like a game
of twenty questions.

OMENS

Today is strange.
Measuring its unusualness
through the number
of black ravens flying
and spiders in the belfry
the commotion of tolling clocks
and brambles of fallen willow.
Senses eerily alerted
to everything odd
and out-of-place.

GHOSTED

Gutted and ghosted
I left you, explanation-less
but it's for your own good
as I am too transient to stay.

THE THING WITH PARTING

Sutures I've let fester from a fallen heart
rallying in the cries
of discarded halos.
Rain-pattering kiss is elixir's antidote.

Death is drinking at the bar
numbing its past life.

Touch's sweet traction
running its course
down
the backs of spines, hair-raising.

Remembering time's discord
codependent on counter-clockwise's
ability of reversal.

Choice.
What delicate burdens
dichotomous ounces of hindsight
we wish we possessed.

A memory.
Stings in ember-ing eyes
ablaze with tear's gravity
panging for future's transpiration.

Rotten floorboards have my foothold
stability's illusion beneath.

Breath's last remorse lets you
float up in heavenly recital—
farewells never liked pomp and circumstance.

Locket you up
captured for an eternity.
a little thing
that took your life away.

THE DIMNESS

We're all operating at different dimness levels
depending on the day.
Denuded branches in
what I believed (at the time)
a sanctuary
of cottonwoods
billowing in the unfaithful sun
casting deep tenor shadows
through the minutia of twigged space
crestfallen by a lapsing season
and an absent left-handed lover
letting them all,
like the light
ever-so slowly
dissipate
dim

disappear.

INKLING FOR FOG

I always had an inkling for fog
piercing its limited-visibility veil
and need-to-know secrets.
Bushwhacking through alder-smacking
beckoning
swan-diving
into a second coming of clarity
dreaming of crossing
snow-white thresholds
of that which I
will never
be able to
truly see
beyond.

WHEN THE FROST ARRIVES

When the frost arrives
I put my arms through a second-hand,
thrifted cross-hatched flannel.
Button by button,
coalescing the sides of this cold-weather shirt
that will be diligently worn
for the foreseeable, snow-filled future.

When the frost arrives
wool socks beg to be darned.
Bare, grass-stained feet nestle into fuzzy fibers
excesses of fleece and fires
enlisted to dutifully keep us from cold's crisp clutch:
the number one priority.

When the frost arrives
the kitchen: a bustling metropolis
of gourmet accomplishments.
Sweet-onion tears:
an essential ingredient in every
Five-star homecooked meal—
togetherness: the garnish.

When the frost arrives
the winter warlock dusts frozen particles onto windowsills,
whimsically.
Despite morning trepidation to face frigid air
we still venture out
to witness woodland's annual dawn magic.

When the frost arrives
we slow
down
(but just a little).

SNOW WHITE AND THE SEVEN PAW PRINTS

Kerfuffle of paw prints, seven
in a powdered bliss
blood
stain on snow
there is no reverence of mass
in animal massacre.

A survival-of-the-fittest sacrifice
so that
someone
or something
may eat.

BELT OF VENUS

Alpenglow has a steady swiftness to it
that never faces reproach.
Jutting freeze breaks
into river's confluence
and I learn what it means to shatter
then submerge
in unforgiving waters.
Feeling more like liability than lover
at this hour—
I'm melting in the belt of Venus
as it douses me in blush
and turns me blue
in an everlasting instant.
Dreaming about the days
of standstill
I'm the please-don't-pick-me girl
wondering why disappointment
always has such a precipitous effect.
Afraid of both my own soul
and ice's impermanence
facing a fork-in-the-road decision paralysis:
right toward a heart heist
or
left on an excursion
for moonlight's resurfacing.

Either way
I am
asunder.

STARLING

I, am
a gross deviation from a starling
but yet there remain similarities
in our simplicities.
Feathered down
whistling out
to you in birdsong.
We, are
just skin and sinew
fate fuming at our flesh
as we fly high
bush-hopping through
something that feels
woolen, and *wanting*
wanting
to weather
this winter
nesting
with
you.

GRAVEYARD GROVE

There is a tale of graveyard grove
and winter's warning gale,
Peak through the birches
There is lake,
Where unrecovered bodies hail.

Graveyard grove, oh graveyard grove
There it takes, oh there she goes
Graveyard grove, oh graveyard grove,
Down to the bottom, oh no.

Through graveyard grove so heavenly white.
A place of beauty, a place of light
But a warning to all
Of a place to fall
Through the ice's deceiving smite.

And on that day, a lone stroll she took
Into the blizzard's sheer might
A jarring lake crack
Balance a-lacked
And she lost control affright.

Polar-shot veins
As she pierced the ice-thin lace,
Into the depths
From one misstep
Goes her pallor-ridden face.

Frigid air accumulates
On this dying December date.
Now she lies at the bottom
Long forgotten
In a stone-cold peaceful state.

BELABORED HOWL

At this point,
I am slated for three hours of sleep
and a long-overdue thirsty Thursday.
It was an ad hoc moment
interpreting lust for love
refraining from reason
on a good run from bad luck—
stuck on small-town trauma.
How many half truths do I tell myself?
Territorial over things not my own
reneging on my tried-and-true typeface
at the townhall
I object to
the tempo of the times
speaking in deft sentences
giving into irrationality,
so irate
by having to grapple with the world
with butter-finger hands.
There's a big difference
in following directions
and setting your own
but as I reach
for the new moon
heads and tails
between my legs
longing
to belong
here
is a belabored howl.

DAYLIGHT'S SAVING

At her funeral,
Gregory Alan Isakov's "If I Go, I'm Goin'" would play on repeat.
The song she chose when her best friend asked:
What song would you commit suicide to?

This house, she's holding secrets…

Medication remnants found on the countertops.
A white-pill powder keg, dosage discrepancy
scattered alongside a newly sharpened salmon filet knife,
a bathtub, lukewarm, when they found her, sunken.
Cherry red cheeks in a pool of crimson.
She was never late for work.
She was late to work that day…

This house, she's quite the talker
She creeks and moans, she keeps me up.

She spoke of her darkness' constant chatter
in journal pages lined now in a cursive induced coma,
wringing out the pain from writhing pen.
A portrayal of the future she was facing
fearing stagnancy in that final stanza.
Writing made her so happy.
Writing eased the pain.

And the photographs know I'm a liar…

Her video-of-the-day montage flashes on the television screen,
documenting the good days
dancing with a sunbeam smile, twirling in the best light.
There's glee, no glimmer of mental illness in sight.
Behind the frame,
out-of-focus, uncentered, press pause.

Maybe someone would have noticed
she admired the height of a bridge.
She was always smiling.
She was scared.

And if I go, I'm goin' crazy

Her will was written
in free verse,
a testament to the reluctance to structure
and necessary legalities.
Spewing apologies in dried ink,
love is something she never quite understood
the interworking's of
feeling so estranged from her own soul.

And if I go I'm goin' shameless

Despite the shame,
she did not relinquish
to her mind's troubled tune.
The vestiges of the past
are on low volume
filled now
solely
of sun's clear instructions
that she must stay.
And,
she makes an unyielding promise
to always experience
daylight's salubrious saving.

THE COLD TRUTH

There's something about small-town dynamics
in a village as tidal as
she is.
Easily persuaded by fiction
smiling over blissful mountain-topped moments
that haven't happened yet.
A rose in a world
of noxious thorns
and wicked integers
waiting impatiently
for someone
to see her through the seasons
before saying
they are *sure as snow*.

Once before
she did not believe
in medicated miracles,
but with the stabilization
of seasonal depression,
the oscillating thermometer
that wavers below zero
no longer has
such a detrimental
December effect.

TO TESSA

A slice of salmonberry cake
and nails in chameleon shades
she's a Brooks-range bandit
Dall sheep kind-of-doll.
Nushagak net-setter, fish-pickin' posse.
Playing freezer roulette of last-season's bounty:
Moose, caribou, ptarmigan, grouse, spruce chicken
home-cooked, home-bodied badass
sleek big-game skulls, reclaimed by resin.
Wood-to-fire, fire-to-steam
we are cleansed in the Yup'ik maqi manner.
Merino wool turtlenecks and mink scrunchies
off-the-road-system stillness seekers—
clickety clack
the ice queens are back.

WHITE AMBIVALENCE

Shaken, not stirred.
She doffed her hat and fastened her penny coat.
The door swelled open with the breath of the blizzard.
Strands and snow departed into *white ambivalence*.

SURFEITS OF SNOW

Surfeits of snow
promenade with wind.
We move at a glacial pace
rendering the boot trudge arduous—
a cumbersome commute.
The village is *slick*.

SINGE

Strewn fairy lights
in riverside bungalows
in the warm glow
I read the finger-stenciled words
on the fogged-up windows.
It was worth it—
I think.
Dog chasing
on riverbanks
flannelled lumberjacks
swinging axes
into knotted timber
to kindle fires that were only
meant to last the winter.
Some things
burn slow
and others—fast
like us.

FLEEING THE HOLD

An out-of-sync
sitting down next to me.
An empty seat
reserved for anybody
but your too-late blizzarding associations.
Deciphering the audacity
of past love's expiry
leg-laced in passivity
I disavow destiny
and all its misgivings
while sporting your stolen
high-school t-shirt
in this takedown of winter.
Wolverine blue banter gone dry
a gut-wrenching get-out-of-here.
My anxiety
such shaky-handed torture
telling me the truth
be told
I'm beside myself
on the bleachers.
Middle fingers out of fucks-to-give
but fumbling with an exit strategy
wrestling with wreaking havoc.
A spotlight exodus—
with everyone watching
in a signature-move two seconds
I decide I have better things to do
than to be pinned
and penned,
yours truly.

FOULING OUT OF A FOOL'S ERRAND

How many take backs do I get in this life?
It's a new year,
but it's all the same 'ol same 'ol
replay of a recurring ending.
Cotton-mouthed lips
and calling you out
someone said the reconstruction
of a heart
takes a labor of love
but I've been benched, slowly dying
on hardwood's constant run in with *what if—*
a behind-the-back play
fouling out of a fool's errand.
Being affixed to aloofness
takes some structural realignment
and getting a grip
is a dangerous overture.
Healing's lineup is already full, so I am
sidelined in stone-cold stoicism.
Finality is one last missed shot and having to
high-five all my angel numbers
for sportsmanship's sake.

For a while,
your memory was something I thought
I had to vanquish,
but now it seems
with such a hard-fought loss
I no longer wish
to keep playing
in such a disappointing game.

ABSOLUTION

Bivouac breakdown
breaking timid trail
the perfect place to pout
is in a frozen flume.
How unnerving it is to heal
to have to retrieve all your archenemies
from the ether—
I find sanctity on a whiteout stroll
with your shadow self.
Finally
love is not a simple helix predicated
on spring's flowery language
and unbeknownst to the willow cinema
I deal a tarot-card truce.
It's steady amortization
turning the clock back to summer
shrinking apertures
of our unlevered coexistence.
I have the courage to greet euphoria
and bend slowly into some semblance of DNA
abandoning last season's capricious aurora
for auspicious alpenglow.
I don't know what forgiveness or four-wheel drive
is supposed to feel like
but apparently,
I'm doing it now
in snowfall's peaceful signage
barreling past your house.
I say that I like the dark now, but
I see that
the light
in your bedroom
is still
on.

FEBRUARY SKY

I haven't had enough of close proximities.
Hands round waists
held like it meant something
you could lose
because you knew you would.
I can't quite tell what it is but
maybe the sun looks different
here in Appalachia.
He insists life is cloudy without me
so I open my draping love
with a window-sill smile
every morning o'er the hills of
his family('s) tree(s)
break down my closed doors
to the studs every time—
I'm worth rebuilding
near those rolling acres
that we are destined to inhabit.
As luck would have it
our eyes bleed recessive blue
hours, not enough of 'em.
Our skin: its own geography
that will go unexplored
for the time being:
Two in transit.
With cheeks like that, unrivaled,
he says he'll never buy me roses
Both: Perennial.
Let's endure—
through dialects
through distance.
How sobering it is to wait patiently
in such an unpretentious manner.

My twang-less voice
offering up who I am
under whiskey's encouragement.
Drinking Crown
Royal enough
for a Kentucky King.
For now
I'll make haiku proclamations
in my place
hoping in 5-7 syllabic months
I'll find myself
amongst Mt. Vernon laurel again
vaguely remembering
that valley stage.
The both of us
in time
better than what we once were
that day
when rainbows plagued
the February sky.

SHEDDING SEASON

I always wore baggy clothes
hated the way fabric clung to me
like the hands of former lovers
in outdated historical fashion
holding on to past tenses
and paternal last
names.

In December's delicate dress
dropping down
like moose antlers:
these articles we must release
naturally.

This skin demands space
this personal label, alleviation
and these things
are merely layers
that we wear
and are finally ready to
shed.

THE CROWDS I RUN IN

I am friends with arbiters of justice, anglers, and the asinine. Single mothers, smokejumpers, the spirited. I am friends with those scraping by and those rollin' in it. The joyous, the jovial, the jocund. I am friends with critters, culprits, creators. The downtrodden, downcast, the depressed. The uplifted, the uplifters. I am friends with dogs and puppies and purr-y specimens. I am friends with the gendered and non-binary. I am friends with shes, hes, theys, and all pronouns-not-yet. I am friends with most, public-enemy number one of a few, but just know that, me and my friends, every once in a while, stay out way past our self-imposed adult curfews. Friends with vices, friends with virtues, friends who always need to use the loo. Gluten-intolerants, vegans, vegetarians, pescatarians, keto friends, friends with their hearts on the mend and on their sleeves. Yeehaw friends, hike-ten-miles-in-the-pouring-rain friends, glitter-wearing friends, bow hunters, beauty queens, skateboarders, skeptics, skiers. Take-me-out-of-my-comfort-zone friends, call-me-out-on-my-bullshit friends. Astrology-lovers, agnostics, arete-adventurers. Ain't-to-cool-to-dance friends, two-left-feet friends. Friends that sing, friends that listen. Friends…now and yet to come, a non-exhaustive list, aforementioned.

SALINAS, CALIFORNIA LETTUCE & GILROY GARLIC

Once upon a time,
the Instagram algorithm got something right.
It pegged two aspiring writers
as suggested friends.

Jace living in Salinas, California—
mecca of fresh produce
or otherwise known as Steinbeck County.
Me in bush Alaska
where the hardiness zone is
not favorable for a long-growing season
necessitating the need for a
subsistence lifestyle.

Jace touts her hometown's lettuce
and that her party trick is correctly guessing
where every item in a grocery store produce section
comes from.
Butter lettuce: From the field
right next to her high school.
Strawberries: Watsonville.
On the other side of the overpass:
Castroville. It has artichokes
along with a sculpture of the town's
highly venerated vegetable.
But, how could she forget the garlic?
The Gilroy *fucking* garlic.

Jace says her state feeds everyone
and I'm convinced.
When I go to my village's sole grocery store
it is winter
and the fresh produce starts to wane
as flights face constant cancellations

from windy weather holds
and below 500-foot cloud ceilings.
Yet I see one last packaged lettuce in
the standing refrigerator
and check the backside
to see its origin: Salinas, CA.

Surely, she does feed the world—
be it lettuce or with her wise words.
I tell her it takes a village
to survive in the bush, but
Salinas lettuce
does a lot of surviving of its own.
It makes a mighty long journey
to get here
slightly distressed from its travels, yet
it is so welcomed.

Even though the lettuce was a little wilted,
a piece of Salinas made it to remote Alaska,
and maybe one day Jace will, too.
So instead, I grab
three semblances of on-sale garlic
and Jace has a flashback about Gilroy
and warns me that
one should never be trapped there
in a car with no air conditioning
when it is 100 degrees Fahrenheit (or above) out.
She says being stuck in the hot garlic valley
makes for a traumatizing childhood memory.
But luckily, the Galiban Range protects
Salinas from the stench.

As a fourth-generation (barely) Italian descendant
I tell her how much I love the smell of garlic
and how such a pungent fate could not be *that* bad.
But Jace has a very niche experience
and I cannot make assumptions on
Gilroy's summer garlicky flavored-air horrors.

But when I read Jace's writing
it tells of all the trauma she has had to overcome
or witness—
I just never thought Gilroy garlic
would be one
of them.

BIG-DIPPER BECKONING

Waxing-gibbous evening
big-dipper beckoning
trail in tungsten greys.
Skiing beside my shadow
there are hundreds of hallelujahs
a million celebrations
and a welcoming of every ounce
of light's exalting extension.

NEVERLAND AT NANCY LAKE

It's neverland at Nancy Lake
a quartet of friends and
disco inferno dreaming on the ceiling.
Rhythmical saw sedation
wood, chopped (in a novice nature)
with gravity's fine efficiency.
Lamplight lessons in card-game gregariousness
and shaky-leg cross-country-ski spl—its
crystalizing this cabin-fever season.

At twenty-three below
stoking the wood-stove's saving grace—
January feels warm once again.

CHUGACH COLOR SCHEMES

Shhh!
The performance has started.
Another winter.
wrinkling my nose in months
of newly excavated hobbies.

A mountain
draped in white-faceted diamonds—
characters in Gore-Tex costumes
costumed (rightfully) for this exact scenery.

Brush-strokes and barreling down in deep precision
a gallery of godly painted landscape canvases
chilled in Chugach color schemes—
this is what well-beings are believed to depend on.

Bowing my head in altitudinal respect
I must be meek if this is the earth I am inheriting.
Holding my fate and fear in this first descent
proceeding with the powder penetration of a millennium
finding the flow-state freedom I once heard of
flying in a lidless sky of bluebirds.

On this day,
the heavens have opened for us
in a true theatrical tenderness
we are brought to tears
by something so beautiful
in what we call our *backyard*.

WINTER SOLSTICE

Insignia of significance
recipients of e x p a n d i n g ethereal darkness
on the precipice of . . .

winter solstice.

Playing in hope's pool of applicants
counting the number of sundials
and sun dogs
collecting the contours
of earth's revolutions
we are lantern-carriers on a quest for
the incoming spring season
slowly reclaiming the days that lay ahead.
Reminiscent rays begin to stretch
into brighter hours
dawn rises
and dusk sets
into the sweet intentions
of our human hearts—

each moment

                                        yielding to light.

SERENDIPITY

And for my life
I have been given
so much serendipity—
enough to save me
tenfold

and then some.

DEAR FUTURE ME

I hope you're blue-hour awakening, alarm-clock-less in Alaska // tea kettle piping a steam whistle // village-special Howdy and black-lab buddy Yeehaw trotting alongside while you complete your daily homestead chores // hand-milking the docile Holstein // easter-egg hunting in the barn for a breakfast scramble // chopping birch straight down the center line, no-knotted clean cuts, slivered kindling for wood-stove's flamed embrace // a chest freezer bulked up with salmon and moose protein // ritualizing dancing-in-the rain baptisms // left-finger rounded with turquoise and wooded band // manuscript and child number three on the way // writing love into the narrative // undaunted by change // unbridled hair lassoing the western wind wilder // be-free breathing fresh starts in a first snowfall // standing atop a jagged mountain peak, cobalt water-coloring the evening cloudless // with a never-departing moonbeam smile // mountaineering to your highest aspirations // and waiting for present me, ever-so patiently, to find you.

ACKNOWLEDGMENTS

To the wondrous watercolor-er, AnnMarie Young, for capturing my western states fireweed cover art perfectly. To Skyler Karajanis, a graphic-design guru, for crafting the scenic art for each seasonal section heading. To Kristina Konstantinova, for formatting and styling this adventurous collection. To the rainbow reminder, no-sad-song-in-the-car rule-maker, about-the-author-photo artist, Nat Stardust. To my editor and much-needed punctuation patroller, Zachary Olson. To my salmon festie bestie with the highest vibe frequency around, Abaigeal O'Brien. To Jace Rowe, the poetic powerhouse from Steinbeck county and algorithm-discovered friend. To the huntress-I-aspire-to-be and soul sister, Tessa Zahradka. To Christina McDermott, for linguistic lessons and the back cover blurb. To all of the folks I have met on this life journey thus far. To all the adventures housed in my memory bank. And most importantly, to the beautiful spaces and places of the West that have led me to where I am today.

ABOUT THE AUTHOR

Lancee is a human. Being. A seeker-of-the-quiet, living in the fireweed-filled spaces of the West. Inspired by roadside daisies and incandescent light, she is a perpetual first draft in pursuit of collecting a mountain of poetic memories. In humble reverence for the spaces of the West that shaped her, Lancee hopes that her poetry plants this same appreciation in her readers as well. May we all positively imprint the land we live on and thank it for all the gifts and wisdom it has shared, and continues to share, with us.